AF335059

Gallery Books
*Editor:* Peter Fallon

# THE DEVIL HIMSELF

John Hughes

# THE DEVIL HIMSELF

Gallery Books

*The Devil Himself*
was first published
simultaneously in paperback
and in a clothbound edition
on 30 April 1996.

The Gallery Press
Loughcrew
Oldcastle
County Meath
Ireland



ISBN 1 85235 185 3 (*paperback*)
      1 85235 186 1 (*clothbound*)

The Gallery Press receives financial assistance from An Chomhairle
Ealaíon / The Arts Council, Ireland, and acknowledges also the assis-
tance of The Arts Council of Northern Ireland in the publication of
this book.

# Contents

*for Sheila O'Donnell*

# The Sons of Noah

When the flood subsided
Noah's three sons left the ark
and set out in different directions
from Mount Ararat
to make their way in the world.

Shem being the laziest of the trio
got no further than the foot of the mountain
and named where he found himself *Asia*.

Japhet being an adventurer
swam the Bosphorus
and, remembering his father's advice,
built a house on stilts
which he called *Europe*.

Ham being a mystic
implored God to lift him
by the scruff of the neck
and set him down wherever he pleased.
When God didn't respond
Ham began worshipping trees
and soon found himself in a land
they called *Africa*.

As for Noah,
to this day he hasn't left the ark
because he's afraid of the sins of the son
being visited upon the father
in any way other than by water.

# The Place Where Engines are Made

I prised open the yellow door to prove her guilt.
But instead of finding a Damascene scimitar
I discovered the Lamb of God
that washes away the sins of the world.

When my ears began to ring
I knew I was in the place where engines are made
only when there is a gibbous moon
and a wind blowing from the east.

As I picked up a Hindoo wrench
the ground gave way beneath me
and the blood of the Lamb trickled down my throat . . .
And so it all began in the confusion of a dream.

# The Stone

I lobbed a stone into the lough
knowing I'd be dead
before it hit the bottom.

Only when God abdicated his throne
did the stone float to the surface
and throw itself ashore.

And if from that day on
the stone is no longer a stone
who can put his hand

where the heart is supposed to be
and say anything other than
'That comes as no surprise to me.'

# The Art of Story-telling

A woman who never listens to her son
doesn't begin his bedtime story
the way he likes stories to begin,

so he becomes his stepfather
and stabs her in the throat
with the sharpest knife in Ireland.

As I'm her guardian angel
he wants to know if it's likely
that in the next world

she'll lecture the grim brothers Grimm
in the art of story-telling
and inflicting jugular wounds.

I pretend not to hear the question
as I jive on the head of the needle
with which she's sewing her own eyes shut.

'My mother would be proud of you'
will be the last words he'll ever utter
to someone he can't see.

# The Emigrant

I murdered my wife in a Statute Acre
of elms and apple trees.

I murdered my daughter in a Cunningham Acre
of birches and oaks.

I murdered my son in a Plantation Acre
of whitethorn and ash.

And because they didn't mean much to me
I smeared their corpses with pitch,

strung them up from a sycamore
and set them all alight.

As the neighbours came running across the fields
I set out for the American colonies —

determined to pass through the Cumberland Gap
in the company of the scum of the earth.

# The Shadow of Levallyreagh

And always he is blinded and buried in a holly-grove
along with a creepie, a bull-roarer,
a thraw-hook, a two-headed axe,
a black-faced lamb, two grains of sand,
a dewy pebble, a cracked plate,
and a wondrously strange type of mushroom.

And always there comes a time in the next world
when he regains his sight.
It is then he weeps at the thought
of snow and wind and winter stars.
It is then he knows himself to be
in the shadow of the shadow of the shadow.

# The Irish Grid

Though the river dried up forty years ago
it is still marked on the quarter-inch map
because the cartographer refuses to believe
his meandering baptismal font, his Jordan,
evaporated as soon as he was immersed in it.

As I explained to the cartographer
the error of his ways
he said he loved me
because I had an evil laugh.

Only then did I stroke his two-headed dog
and step outside to be eaten by the wind
at J23 53 on the Irish Grid.

# Diesel

One blue mountain road zigs and the other zags
before they entwine to become the road
to Jack Gallagher's MS station.

Driving along that road in a chunky 4 x 4 —
on my way to buy gallon upon gallon of diesel
and half a hundredweight of Blues and Pinks —

I listened to the devils' stories
about Ardoyne, Iberian griffins, desert frost,
and bishops who sweat semen in their sleep.

It was driving Kerrys and Jerseys along the same road
that the angels told my grandfather
stories about the fifth apostle and Munster Simms.

When the angels disappeared behind a Famine wall
my grandfather coughed up his ravaged lungs
and threw them to the winged lion

that had been stalking him for fifty years —
from the time he set fire to a Red Kelly barn
built to store the fleece of the Lamb of God.

The lion swooped down on me
as I poured gallon upon gallon of diesel
over the Blues and the Pinks, the devils and the angels.

# People in the House

Anyone who is chased into the house
will be afraid to touch its walls
because the light-bulb hanging from the ceiling
illuminates nothing but itself.

Let me tell you that in the house
there is always a poisonous plant
growing out of someone's breast-pocket.

As I sleep snow falls over the house
and the blue of my dreams isn't that of the sky,
or that of the flowers that sell their gardeners,
or that of the suits that sell their tailors.

Perhaps it's winter nowhere else but the house,
and the twilight is the blue of my dreams.

*after the Romanian of Grigore Balanescu*

# The Number of No Return

Between the grave of a dog and the den of a fox
the sulphurous embers glowed for a month.
In that time I placed an obol in my mouth
and ate the heads and tails of Cerberus
to be sure I'd never become a rich man
who could afford to buy the last thing he ever saw —
that being the bridge made of human hair and bone
which crosses the Styx at its widest point.

That I failed will come as no surprise
to the Pope in Avignon and the pretender in Rome,
for only they know the significance
of the embers being in the shape of a six —
the number I will not count beyond
for fear of discovering what follows it
is not called seven
and *is* called the number of no return.

# Leaving Home

The day I threw my head up and left home
my mother told me the facts of life:

Catholicism is based on opium
and mutual masturbation,

the Garden of Eden is submerged
beneath the Caspian Sea,

the Holy Ghost was born in County Offaly,

from Cape Verde to the Cape of Good Hope
all exchanges and valuations of merchandise
are made on the foot of the macoute,

the pygmies of Thrace are born aged five
and die aged eight.

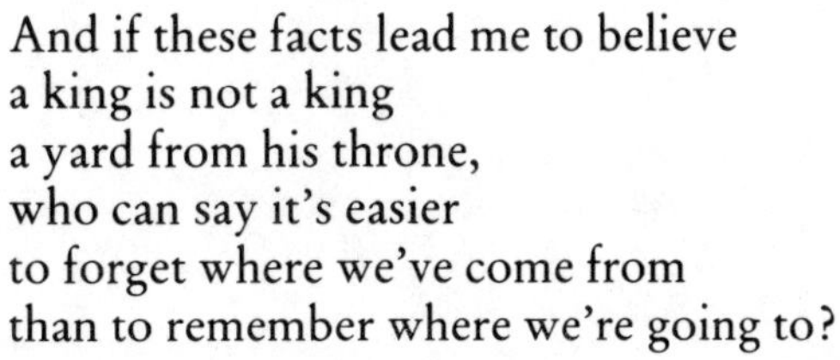

And if these facts lead me to believe
a king is not a king
a yard from his throne,
who can say it's easier
to forget where we've come from
than to remember where we're going to?

# The Bishops of Clogher

On the night of the Last Judgement
twelve Bishops of Clogher congregated
on the steps of Kitty Cambric's Tavern
to take the oath of allegiance
to the Queen of the Queens of God.

According to Stendhal
all but one of the bishops
then retired to Mother Clap's Molly House
to enjoy the favours of the Son of God
and eleven of his twelve disciples.

# Dragonwyck of Burgoyne

Through the emptiness of Great Syria and Palestine
she walked, and walked, and walked, did Dragonwyck
whose suit of armour was swathed in silk
and whose sword had never fallen on the heads
of Partheys, Wargers, Ventadorms, or Bahrangurs.
And all the while Dragonwyck sang,
'Know then, whoever ye may be, that without this sword
I am no more than a troubling dream to myself.'

Only when Dragonwyck reached Golgotha
did she regret the lack of blood upon her one good hand.
And when the King of the Jews instructed her to open her mouth
the sky turned black and the never-ending wind,
known by only one of its thousand thousand names,
began to blow life into the archangel who'd perished
twisting his sword into the belly of the virgin
pregnant with the King of the Jews.

Through the emptiness of the Sinai and Egypt
she walked, and walked, and walked, did Dragonwyck
whose silk evening-gown was in tatters
and whose mouth was full of blood and semen —
toward her death at the huge and trembling hands of a shepherd
wonderful for his knowledge of her journey
toward her death at the huge and trembling hands of a shepherd
watching over the liver and heart of the Paschal Lamb.

# The Howling

And at night, within sight of The Rose Tower, she'd rise from her grave. Every dog she'd ever stroked howled till daybreak. But the villagers never heard a thing because they were in a deep sleep — dreaming they were sleep-walking through the Pavilion of the Old Moon during the Ching Dynasty under the rule of the Emperor Ch'ien Lung. It was left to strangers to comment upon the howling dogs before being thrown to them by me.

# Eckhart's Road

As soon as time had stopped standing still
and made up for what it had lost of itself
Meister Eckhart — he of the fir-cone breath —
brought me to the fork in the road,
half-way between my cradle and his grave,
where I'd first told him the discrepancies
between his dreams and his dreambooks
were not my responsibility.

As I listened to the wind
(the oldest story-teller of them all)
explain why *Mistral* was its favourite name
the road went behind my back to sell Eckhart
its treacherous twists and turns
to the so-called ends of the earth,
where the last step may as well be the first
of another journey altogether.

# 1812

When I tried to hold onto the wind
with my rotten teeth
my horse took fright and bolted.

As soon as I lost sight of it
two corporals of Napoleon's Grand Army
slaughtered it for lunch and dinner.

After he'd studied the fly-blown carcass,
downwind and from twenty metres off,
the local savant calculated
the soldiers had eaten
seven per cent of the animal.

Why does it give me pleasure to say
it was snowing the day
I set out for Moscow
to lay the horse's skull
at the emperor's swollen feet?

# Atop the Ghat

The younger of two bo'suns
lectures the older of two captains
on the nature of George III's lunacy.

The ghost of my great-grandfather
burns his Stuyvesant leg
and a devil's dozen of Stars and Stripes.

I watch the *Half-Moon on the Hudson*,
manned by a deathly-pale crew,
transport a cargo of movable feasts
as far west as is wise to imagine.

# Jonah

The whaler fell overboard
and was swallowed by his quarry.
He lit a fire in the True Whale's belly
and waited for nature to take its course.

Somehow he kept himself alive for a year,
hacking his way out of the whale
when it beached itself
on our western shore.

As soon as every islander
had heard his story sixty-six times
I suggested he make his way to the mainland
where such a story would be thought a fable.

On the stormy crossing to the mainland
he revealed his true identity
and requested we throw him overboard.

When we said we didn't have the heart
he jumped into the eye of the storm
and never was seen by us again.

# The Great Bear

The 23rd of September went quiet
when AM stepped out of the mangled car
and into the darkness of a pine forest.

She followed the straight path of the dead
until she entered a scorched clearing
in which a bear had dug seven graves.

AM prostrated herself before the bear
and begged forgiveness for coming upon him
without a knife to cut out his soul.

Then there came a night of rain
that washed away the forest of pines
and the seven graves of seven stars.

# Fate

In the dead of night
I brought a dead crow home to my mother.
She nailed it to the wall
and summoned the prophet Isaiah
to tell him I was possessed
by a demon called Asmodeus.

When the prophet called her
a superstitious fool
she said my fate was open to doubt
and locked me in the cellar
with an armless Croatian angel
who kept saying he didn't care
if tomorrow never came.

I was reconciled to my fate.
That is, I was certain I loved the angel
for all the wrong reasons.

# The Metaphysics of Light

A power-cut had sent me to bed early
the Good Friday I dreamt Shemkel —
the seventh and darkest angel —
had blown the trumpet loud and clear
when the ashes he'd scattered
on my mother's grave
were eaten by Robert Grosseteste's
second-best milker.

And even though I woke up then
the dream didn't end there,
but continued with the cow
climbing the only ash in Aughisnafin
to watch my mother turn in her coffin —
buried in the blackest soil in Ireland —
at the thought of the resurrection
and the inevitable light.

# Blood

When I said she smelt of a lamb and a wolf
she coughed up the field she was born in.
I knew she believed me to be Christ of March 25th.

How often have I walked through the town of Dungiven
flanked by a wolf-headed lamb and a lamb-headed wolf —
the blood coming from their wounds mine and mine alone?

# The Triangle

In a triangle he drew in his sleep
the demon Belphegor pours tar into shoes
while his daughter burns cherubim and seraphim.

She hums with pleasure as he climbs a red ladder
into the darkness of an angle
even demons must fear.

And when Belphegor fails to return —
to poke the charred wings of cherubim and seraphim
with his goat-headed staff —

his daughter wraps the triangle in brown paper
and buries it where the wind from County Armagh
is the wind from California.

# The Devil Himself

After Saint Michael buries his sword of jade
between the motorway and the Burmah station
he'll screech like a newborn and tell me
I am his strangest enemy since Saint Paul.

Then I'll raise Solomon from his grave
among the rocks and rushes and abandoned cars
to ask him if it was true Our Lord had laughed —
for the first time since the Crucifixion —

when I prevailed on the wind to eviscerate
the Lord Panjandrums of Fermanagh and Tyrone
as they cut through Belfast's Marrow Bone
in search of an unbloodied butcher's apron.

Though grateful to be in evil company
Solomon will say the question is beyond one
who thinks the jackal a symbol of Thrones,
Principalities, Dominions, and Powers.

I am afraid I will sob through the eternal night
it will take Solomon to pass judgement
on Our Lord who forgives us all our sins
and is the Devil himself.

# Against the Grain

And because you had traces of me
on your hands, nose, nipples and tongue,
your shadow was taken from you
and replaced with a translucent light.

Brooding on the last words to pass between us —
'Hail Mary, full of shit' —
I waited for you to stink to high heaven
before making the journey to Fintragh Beach.

As the tide went out I held up to the light
a trillion grains of sand
and saw you in all but one of them.
O to be filled with such love and terror.

# Tyrone Gothic

A girl in a white muslin dress
holds a pistol to the head
of her grandmother's corpse.

Downstairs the maid is forced to watch
the master and the mistress masturbate.

In the stables an imbecile prays for Satan
to take the shape of a rabid wolf.

A stranger sits in the family crypt
and wonders if his tragic news
should be delivered at dawn or dusk.

# Day One

You'd taken your eyes off the road
to stare at the dead fox and dying dog
lying in the passenger-seat

when your old Ford left the road
and somersaulted three times
into the electric blueness of the Sphinx Pool.

As the rain lashed down
and the Angel of Death debated with himself
whether or not to inspect your corpse

the car sank to the bottom of the pool —
the sound of which was said to be like
the Angel of Death muttering to himself

about old dreams of Kalashnikovs,
Armalites, Walthers, Thompsons, Uzis,
two-headed angels and devils with many wings.

# The Hunt

In the far north of the country
a young wolf attacked me for good reason.

As suddenly as it had come out of the west
it disappeared into the east.

I survived to be hunted down by a wolf next year
as I've been ever since I deserted the pack

in the six hundredth year of Noah's life,
in the second month, on the seventeenth day.

# Mary-Celeste

It took all of June for us to reach
latitude 22° north,
longitude 23° west.

At that position
Mary-Celeste threw the King James Bible
over the starboard side
and began speaking in tongues.

When she lost her voice
she dived from the crow's nest
and swam around the ship ninety-seven times.

When she climbed back on board
I held a knife to my throat
and threatened to scuttle the ship
unless she explained why we were where we were.

It took all of July
for us to reach
the bottom of the sea.

# Saint George and the Dragon

When she refused to lie beneath me
I threw her behind a tapestry
which depicted an almost invisible Saint George
slaying a still vivid dragon.

Only when that sickliest sweet of smells
filled the house from top to bottom
could I rest easy enough
to dream of her still lying beneath me.

O that I could say
I woke up at the crack of dawn
to find that smell still there
and Saint George as vivid as his prey.

# The Blind Leading the Blind

Because a barefoot Saint Paul
passed us on Damascus Street
without a nod or a wink
we'll be able to close our eyes
in the sure and certain knowledge
the darkness we're in
is ours and ours alone.

# The Black Wind

As soon as I stopped fulminating
against the black wind from Siberia
John Joseph pulled up a chair to the fire
and told me he'd dreamt of a long silence
which was broken by the sound
of a door locking itself against the dark.

I told him that he must forget the dream
when he returned home to discover
his dogs lying quiet in the yard
and his daughter hanging from a tree.
When John Joseph turned his back on me
I hissed like a wet stick in the fire.
In the cold dawn I cried crocodile tears
when he asked how it was I knew so little.

# Pegasus Walk

I fall to my knees on Pegasus Walk
and listen for the sound of hoofs
or the swish swoosh swoosh of wings.

I know that he may pass by so quietly,
or so far overhead, I'll not hear him.
If that happens I'll eat a stone garnished with basil

and then open a box which contains a box
which contains a box which contains
a walking-stick and a winged horse.

The silence is the silence of a place
where every man, woman, and cat-headed dog
has gone to sit by Death's deathbed.

# The Ashes of Bohemia

As I've been staring at the *O* in Bohemia
I close the atlas, dress for death,
and leave the house ablaze.

I walk through the quagmire that is the garden
and clamber over eleven red gates
to watch three mastiffs tear a badger limb from limb.

When she opens the atlas at Bohemia
she finds it stained with the sweat
of one who believes that he might be me.

She closes her eyes to see him
throwing rocks at the dying badger
as the mastiffs feed on their own guts.

The night wind blows upon Bohemia
as I open the charred door to our house
and am overcome by our foul stench.

I come to on a bed of sticks and stones
floating down a pencil-thin river
toward the *O* in Bohemia.

Tomorrow being another day of mysteries
I will still be travelling
toward the smoke, the embers, and the ashes of Bohemia.

# Notes

*page* 15 A Statute Acre is also known as an English Acre (as used today). A Cunningham Acre is also known as a Scotch Acre and equals 1.29 statute acres. A Plantation Acre is also known as an Irish Acre and equals 1.62 statute acres.

*page* 16 Levallyreagh: A townland near Finnis, Co. Down.

*page* 22 'The Bishops of Clogher' was Stendhal's phrase for homosexuals — after a Bishop of that diocese was found in the tender embraces of a soldier.